MONAS H

('THE HIEROGLYPHIC MONAD')

by Dr. JOHN DEE

Antwerp, 1564.

Translated by J.W. Hamilton-Jones, 1947.

To the most excellent Majesty of the famous King Maximilian

[Dee's preface dedicated to Maximilian omitted by J.W. Hamilton-Jones.]

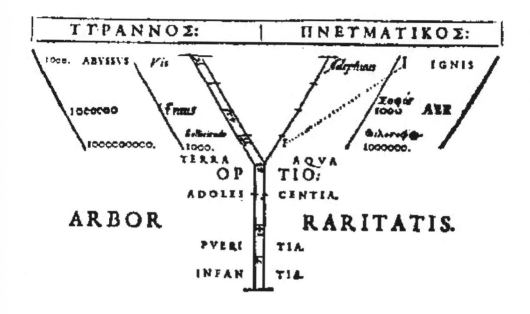

THEOREM I

It is by the straight line and the circle that the first and most simple example and representation of all things may be demonstrated, whether such things be either non-existent or merely hidden under Nature's veils.

THEOREM II

Neither the circle without the line, nor the line without the point, can be artificially produced. It is, therefore, by virtue of the point and the Monad that all things commence to emerge in principle.

That which is affected at the periphery, however large it may be, cannot in any way lack the support of the central point.

THEOREM III

Therefore, the central point which we see in the centre of the hieroglyphic Monad produces the Earth, round which the Sun, the Moon, and the other planets follow their respective paths. The Sun has  the supreme dignity, and we represent him by a circle having a visible centre.

THEOREM IV

Although the semicircle of the Moon is placed above the circle of the Sun and would appear to be superior, nevertheless we know that the Sun is ruler and King. We see that the Moon in her shape and her proximity rivals the Sun with her grandeur, which is apparent to ordinary men, yet the face, or a semi-sphere of the Moon, always reflects the light of the Sun. It desires so much to be impregnated with solar rays and to be transformed into Sun that at times it disappears completely from the skies and some days after reappears, and we have represented her by the figure of the Horns (Cornucopia).

THEOREM V

And truly I give the completion of the idea of the solar circle by adding a semicircle for the Moon, for the morning and the evening were the first day, and it was therefore in the first (day) that the Light of the Philosophers was made (or produced).

THEOREM VI

We see here that the Sun and the Moon are supported upon the right-angled Cross. This Cross may signify very profoundly, and for sufficient reasons in our hieroglyph, either the Ternary or the Quaternary. The Ternary is made by the two straight lines having a copulative centre.

The Quaternary is produced by the four straight lines enclosing four right angles. Either of these elements, the lines or the right angles, repeated twice, therefore, afford us in the most secret manner the Octad, which I do not believe was known to our predecessors, the Magi, and which you should study with great attention. The threefold magic of the first Fathers and the wise men consisted in Body, Soul and Spirit. Therefore, we have here the first manifested Septenary, that is to say, two straight lines with a common point which make three, and the four lines which converge to form the central point in separating the first two.

THEOREM VII

The Elements being far from their accustomed places, the homogeneous parts are dislocated, and this a man learns by experiment, for it is along the straight lines that they return naturally and effectively to these same places. Therefore, it will not be absurd to represent the mystery of the four Elements, in which it is possible to resolve each one into elementary form, by four straight lines running in four contrary directions from one common and indivisible point. Here you will notice particularly that the geometricians teach that a line is produced by the displacement of a point: we give notice that it must be the same here, and for a similar reason, because our elementary lines are produced by a continual cascade of droplets as a flux in the mechanism of our magic.

THEOREM VIII

Besides, the kabbalistic extension of the Quaternary according to the common formula of notation (because we say one, two, three, and four) is an abridged or reduced form of the Decad. This is because Pythagoras was in the habit of saying: 1+2+3+4 make 10. It is not by chance that the right-angled Cross -- that is to say, the twenty-first letter of the Roman alphabet, which was considered as being formed by four straight lines -- was taken by the most ancient of the Roman Philosophers to represent the Decad.

Further, they have defined the place where the Ternary conducts its force into the Septenary.

THEOREM IX

We see that all this accords perfectly with the Sun and Moon of our Monad, because, by the magic of the four Elements, an exact separation upon their original lines must be made; following which the circulatory conjunction within the solar complement through the peripheries of these same lines is performed, because however long a given line may be, it is possible to describe a circle passing through its extremes, following the laws of the geometricians. Therefore, we cannot deny how useful the Sun and the Moon are to our Monad, in conjunction with the decadal proportion of the Cross.

THEOREM X

The following figure of the zodiacal sign Aries ⌒, in use amongst the astronomers, is the same for all the world (a sort of erection both cutting and pointed), and it is understood that it indicates the origin of the fiery triplicity in that part of the sky.

LVNA.

SOL.

ELEMENTA.

IGNIS.

Therefore, we have added the astronomical sign Aries to signify that in the practice of this Monad the use of fire is required.

We finish the brief hieroglyphic consideration of our Monad, which we would sum up in one only hieroglyphic context:

The Sun and the Moon of this Monad desire that the Elements in which the tenth proportion will flower, shall be separated, and this is done by the application of Fire.

THEOREM XI

The mystical sign of the Ram, composed of two semicircles connected by one common point, is very justly attributed to the place of the equinoctial nycthemeron, because the period of twenty-four hours divided by means of the equinox denotes most secret proportions.

This I have said in respect of the Earth.

THEOREM XII

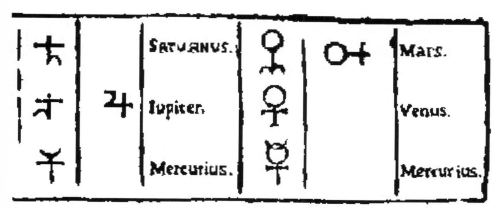

The very ancient wise men and Magi have transmitted to us five hieroglyphical signs of the planets, all of which are composed out of the signs used for the Moon and the Sun, together with the sign of the Elements and the hieroglyphical sign of Aries, the Ram, which will become apparent to those who examine these figures:

Each one of these signs will not be difficult to explain according to the hieroglyphical manner in view of our fundamental principles, already posited. To begin with, we will speak in paraphrases of those which possess the characteristics of the Moon: following that, of those which possess a solar character. When our lunar nature, by the science of the Elements, had accomplished the first revolution round our Earth, then it was called, mystically, Saturn.

Afterwards, at the following revolution, it was named Jupiter, and holds a very 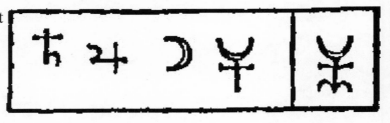 secret figure. Then the Moon, developed by yet a third journey, was represented very obscurely again by this figure which it was their custom to call Mercury . You see how this is Lunar. That it must be conducted through a fourth revolution will not be contrary to our most secret design, whatever certain sages may say. In this manner the pure magical spirit, by its spiritual virtue, will perform the work of the albification at the place of the Moon; to us alone and as it were in the middle of a natural day he will speak hieroglyphically without words, introducing and imprinting these four geogonic figures in the pure Earth very simply prepared by us: this last figure being in the middle of all the others.

THEOREM XIII

Now regard the mystical character of Mars! Is it not formed from the hieroglyphs of the Sun and Aries, the magistery of the Elements partly intervening? And that of Venus -- I wish to know is it not produced from that of the Sun and the Elements according to the best exponents? Therefore, the planets look towards the solar periphery and the work of revivification.

In the progression we will notice this other Mercury ☿ will
appear who is truly the twin brother of the first: for by the
complete Lunar and Solar magic of the Elements, the Hieroglyph
of this Messenger speaks to us very distinctly, and we should
examine it carefully and listen to what it says. And (by the Will of
God) it is the Mercury of the Philosophers, the greatly celebrated
microcosm and ADAM. Therefore, some of the most expert were
inclined to place him in a position of, and give him a rank equal
to, the Sun himself.

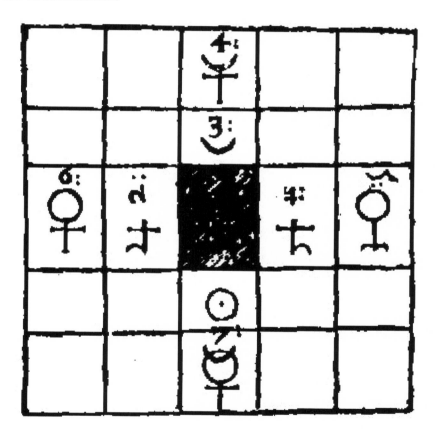

This we cannot perform in the present epoch unless we add to this
coraline crystal work a certain SOUL separated from the body by
the pyrognomic art. It is very difficult to accomplish this and very
perilous because of the fire and the sulphur which the breath
contains within it. But certainly this Soul can perform marvellous

things. For example, join it by indissoluble ties to the disc of the Moon (or at least of Mercury) by Lucifer and Fire. In the third place, it is necessary that we should show (in order to demonstrate our Septenary number) that it is the Sun of Philosophers itself. You will observe the exactitude as well as the clarity with which this anatomy of our Hieroglyphic Monad corresponds to what is signified in the arcana of these two theorems.

THEOREM XIV

It is therefore clearly confirmed that the whole magistery depends upon the Sun and the Moon. Thrice Greatest Hermes has repeatedly told us this in affirming that the Sun is its father and the Moon is its mother: and we know truly that the red earth (*terra lemnia*) is nourished by the rays of the Moon and the Sun which exercise a singular influence upon it.

THEOREM XV

We suggest, therefore, that Philosophers should consider the action of the Sun and the Moon upon the Earth. They will notice that when the light of the Sun enters Aries, then the Moon, when she enters the next sign, that is to say Taurus, receives a new dignity in the light and is exalted in that sign in respect of her natural virtues. The Ancients explained this proximity of the luminaries -- the most remarkable of all -- by a certain mystic sign under the name of the Bull. It is very certain that it is this exaltation of the Moon to which in their treatises the astronomers from the most ancient times bear witness. This mystery can be understood only by those who have become the Absolute Pontiffs of the Mysteries. For the same reason they have said that Taurus is the house of Venus -- that is to say, of conjugal love, chaste and prolific, for nature rejoices in nature, as the great Ostanes concealed in his most secret mysteries. These exaltations are acquired by the Sun, because he himself, after having undergone many eclipses of his light, received the force of Mars, and is said to be exalted in this same house of Mars which is our Ram (Aries).

This most secret mystery is clearly and perfectly shown in our Monad by the hieroglyphic figure of Taurus, which is here represented, and by that of Mars, which we have indicated in Theorem

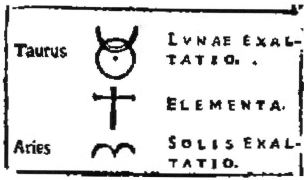

XII and Theorem XIII by the Sun joined to a straight line towards the sign of Aries.

In this theory another kabbalistic analysis of our Monad offers itself, because the true and ingenius explanation is this: the exaltations of the Moon and of the Sun ate made by means of the science of the Elements.

Note. -- There are two things which should be particularly observed: first, that the hieroglyphic figure of Taurus is the same as the diphthong of the Greeks ♉ [i.e. -ou], which was always used in terminating the singular gender; secondly, that by a simple transposition of place we show the letter alpha twice, by a circle and a half-circle, being simply tangents which touch one another as shown.

THEOREM XVI

We must now, in view of our subject, philosophise for a short time upon the Cross. Our Cross may be formed of two straight lines (as we have said) which are equal one to the other -- that is to say, we cannot separate the lines except we do it by parting them so that we get equal lengths. But in the mystic distribution of the components of our Cross, we wish to use parts which are both equal and unequal. These parts show that a virtue is hidden under the power of the division of the Equilateral Cross into two parts, because they are of equal grandeur. In general, the Cross must be composed of equal right angles, since the nature of justice demands the perfect equality of the lines used in the decussation. In accordance with this justice, we propose to examine with care that which follows concerning the Equilateral Cross (which is the twenty-first letter of the Latin alphabet).

If, through the common point where the opposite angles meet in our Rectilineal, Rectangular, and Equilateral Cross, we imagine a straight line dividing it into two parts, then on either side of the line thus traversed we find the parts are perfectly equal and similar. And these parts are similar in shape to that letter of the Romans which is regarded as the fifth of the vowels, and which was frequently used by the most ancient Latin philosophers to represent the number five.

This, I conceive, was not done by them without good reason, because it is in fact the exact half of our Decad. Of these parts of the figure thus duplicated by the hypothetical division of the Cross, we must conclude it to be reasonable that each part represents the quinary, although one is upright and the other reversed in imitation of the multiplication of the square root which comes in here in a marvellous way as the circular number, that is to say, the quinary, from which we find the number twenty-five is produced (because this letter is the twentieth of the alphabet and the fifth of the vowels).

We will now consider another aspect of this same Equilateral Cross -- that which follows is based upon the position shown in our Monadic Cross. Let us suppose a similar division of the Cross into two parts be made as in the drawing.

Now we see the germinating shape of another letter of the Latin alphabet -- the one upright, the other reversed and opposite. This letter is used (after the ancient custom of the Latins) to represent the number fifty. From this, it seems to me, we establish our Decad of the Cross, for this is placed at the summit of all the mysteries, and it follows that this Cross is the hieroglyphic sign of perfection. Therefore, enclosed within the quinary force is the power of the Decad, out of which comes the number fifty as its own product.

Oh, my God, how profound are these mysteries! and the name E L is given to this letter! And for this very reason, we see that it responds to the decadal virtue of the Cross, because, starting from the first letter of the alphabet, L is the tenth letter, and counting backwards from the letter X, we find that it falls into the tenth place, and since we show that there are two parts of the Cross, and considering now their numerical virtue, it is quite clear how the number one hundred is produced. And if by the law of squares these two parts be multiplied together, they give a product of 2500. This square compared with the square of the first circular number, and applied to it, gives a difference of one hundred, which is the Cross itself explained by the square of its Decad, and is recognised as one hundred. Therefore, as this is contained within the figure of the Cross, it also represents unity. By the study of these theories of the Cross, the most dignified of all, we are thereby induced to utilise this progression, viz. one -- ten -- one hundred, and this is the decadal proportion of the Cross as it appears to us.

THEOREM XVII

After a due study of the sixth theorem it is logical to proceed to a consideration of the four right angles in our Cross, to each one of which, as we have shown in the preceding theorem, we attribute the significance of the quinary according to the first position in which they are placed, and in transposing them to a new position, the same theorem shows that they become hieroglyphic signs of the number fifty. It is quite evident that the Cross is vulgarly used to indicate the number ten, and further, it is the twenty-first letter, following the order of the Latin alphabet, and it is for this reason that the sages amongst the Mecubales designated the number twenty-one by this same letter. In fact, we can give a very simple consideration to this sign to find out what other qualitative and quantitative virtues it possesses. From all these facts we see that we may safely conclude, by the best kabbalistic computation, that our Cross, by a marvellous metamorphosis, may signify for the Initiates two hundred and fifty-two. Thus: four times five, four times fifty, ten, twenty-one and one, which added together make two hundred and fifty-two. We can extract this number by two other methods as we have already shown: we recommend to the Kabbalists who have not yet made experiments to produce it, not only to study it in its conciseness, but also to form a judgment worthy of philosophers in regard to the various permutations and ingenious productions which arise from the magistery of this number. And I will not hide from you a further memorable mystagogy: consider that our Cross, containing so many ideas, conceals two further letters if we examine carefully their numerical virtues after a certain manner, so that, by a parallel method following their verbal force with this same Cross, we recognise with supreme admiration that it is from here that LIGHT is derived (LUX), the final word of the magistery, by the union and conjunction of the Ternary within the unity of the Word.

THEOREM XVIII

From our Theorems XII and XIII it may be inferred that celestial astronomy is the source and guide of the inferior astronomy. Before we raise our eyes to heaven, kabbalistically illuminated by the contemplation of these mysteries, we should perceive very exactly the construction of our Monad as it is shown to us not only in the LIGHT but also in life and nature, for it discloses explicitly, by its inner movement, the most secret mysteries of this physical analysis. We have contemplated the heavenly and divine functions of this celestial Messenger, and we now apply this co-ordination to the figure of the egg. It is well known that all astrologers teach that the form of the orbit traversed by a planet is circular, and because the wise should understand by a hint, it is thus that we interpret it in the hieroglyph shown, which conforms in every detail with all that has gone before.

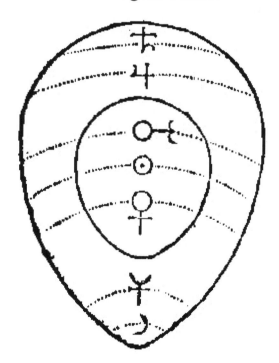

Here you will note that the miserable alchemists must learn to recognise their numerous errors and to understand what is the water of the white of egg, what is the oil of the yoke of egg, and what we mean by calcined egg-shells. These inexpert impostors must learn in their despair to understand what are meant by these and many other similar expressions. Here we have shown almost all the proportions which correspond to Nature herself. This is the same Eagle's Egg which the scarab formerly broke because of the injury which the cruelty and violence of this bird caused to timid and primitive man, for this bird pursued some of them who were running to the cavern where the scarab dwelt, to implore his aid. The scarab wondered in what manner he alone could revenge such insolence, and, being of an ardent character, prepared to accomplish his purpose by constancy and determination, for he was short of neither power nor intelligence. The scarab pursued the eagle resolutely and made use of this very subtle trick: he let fall his ordure in the bosom of Jupiter where the egg was deposited, with the result that the God in getting rid of it threw the egg to the ground, where it was broken. The scarab by this method would have completely exterminated the whole family of eagles from the Earth had not Jupiter, in order to avoid such a calamity, resolved that, during that part of the year when the eagles watch over their eggs, no scarab should come flying near them. Therefore, I counsel those who are ill-treated by the cruelty of this bird, that they learn the very useful art from these solar insects (Heliocantharis) who live concealed and hidden for very long periods of time. By these indications and signs, for which they should be very thankful, they themselves will be able to take vengeance on their enemy. And I affirm (O King!) that it is not Aesop but Oedipus who prompts me, for he presented these things to worthy souls, and ventured for the first time to speak of these supreme mysteries of Nature. I know perfectly well that there have been certain men who, by the art of the scarab, have dissolved the eagle's egg and its shell with pure albumen and have formed thereby a mixture of all; afterwards they have reduced this mixture to a yellow liquid, by a notable process, viz. by a ceaseless circulation just as the scarabs roll their balls of earth.

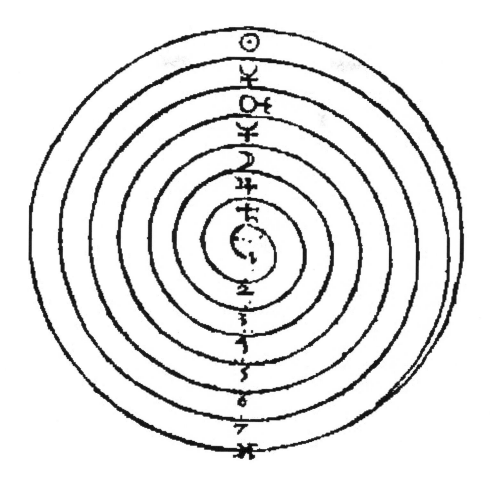

By this means the great metamorphosis of the egg was accomplished; the albumen was absorbed during a great many revolutions round the heliocentric orbits, and was enveloped in this same yellow liquid. The hieroglyphic figure shown here, of this art, will not displease those who are familiar with Nature.

We read that during the early centuries, this art was much celebrated amongst the most serious and ancient Philosophers, as being certain and useful. Anaxagoras performed the magistery and extracted therefrom an excellent medicine, as you may read in his book.

He who devotes himself sincerely to these mysteries will see clearly that nothing is able to exist without the virtue of our hieroglyphic Monad.

THEOREM XIX

The Sun and the Moon shed their corporeal forces upon the bodies of the inferior Elements, much more so than all the other planets. It is this fact which shows, in effect, that in the pyrognomic analysis all metals lose the aqueous humour of the Moon as well as the igneous liquor of the Sun, by which all corporeal, terrestrial, and mortal things are sustained.

THEOREM XX

We have shown sufficiently that for very good reasons the Elements are represented in our Hieroglyph by the straight lines, therefore we give a very exact speculation concerning the point which we place in the centre of our Cross. This point cannot by any means be abstracted from our Ternary. Should anyone who is ignorant of this divine learning, say that in this position of our Binary the point can be absent, we reply, he may suppose it to be absent, but that which remains without it will certainly not be our Binary; for the Quaternary is immediately manifested, because by removing the point we discontinue the unity of the lines. Now, our adversary may suppose that by this argument we have reconstructed our Binary; that in fact our Binary and our Quaternary are one and the same thing, according to this consideration, which is manifestly impossible. The point must of necessity be present, because with the Binary it constitutes our Ternary, and there is nothing that can be substituted in its place. Meanwhile he cannot divide the hypostatic property of our Binary without nullifying an integral part of it. Thus it is demonstrated that it must not be divided. All the parts of a line are lines. This is a point, and this confirms our hypothesis. Therefore, the point does not form part of our Binary and yet it forms part of the integral form of the Binary. It follows that we must take notice of all that is hidden within this hypostatic form and understand that there is nothing superfluous in the linear dimension of our Binary. But because we see that these dimensions are common to both lines, they are considered to receive a certain secret image from this Binary. By this we demonstrate here that the Quaternary is concealed within the Ternary. O God! pardon me if I have sinned against Thy Majesty in revealing such a great mystery in my writings which all may read, but I believe that only those who are truly worthy will understand.

We therefore continue to expound the Quaternary of our Cross as we have indicated. Seek diligently to discover whether the point may be removed from the position in which we first find it. The mathematicians teach that it may be displaced quite simply. At the moment when it is separated the Quaternary remains, and it becomes much more clear and distinct to the eyes of all.

This is not a part of its substantial proportions, but only the confused and superfluous point which is rejected and removed.

O Omnipotent Divine Majesty, how we Mortals are constrained to confess what great Wisdom and what ineffable mysteries reside in the Law which Thou hast made! Through all these points and these letters the most sublime secrets, and terrestrial arcane mysteries, as well as the multiple revelations of this unique point, now placed in the Light and examined by me, can be faithfully demonstrated and explained. This point is not superfluous within the Divine Trinity, yet when considered, on the other hand, within the Kingdom of the four Elements it is black, therefore corruptible and watery. O thrice and four times happy, the man who attains this (almost copulative) point in the Ternary, and rejects and removes that sombre and superfluous part of the Quaternary, the source of vague shadows. Thus after some effort we obtain the white vestments brilliant as the snow.

Oh, Maximilian! May God, through this mystagogy, make you or some other scion of the House of Austria the most powerful of all when the time comes for me to remain tranquil in Christ, in order that the honour of His redoubtable name may be restored within the abominable and intolerable shadows hovering above the Earth. And now for fear that I myself should say too much I shall immediately return to the burden of my task, and because I have already terminated my discourse for those whose gaze is centred within the heart, it is now necessary to translate my words for those whose heart is centred within their eyes. Here, therefore, we can represent in some measure in the figure of the Cross that which we have already said. Two equal lines are equally and inequally crossed through the point of necessity which you see in A.

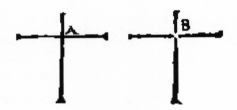

The four straight lines, as in B, produce a sort of vacuum where they are withdrawn from the central point, which was their common condition, in which state they were not prejudical, the one to the other. This is the path by which our Monad, progressing through the Binary and the Ternary into the purified Quaternary, is reconstituted within itself, united in equal proportions, and which now shows that the whole is equal to its combined parts, for during the time that this takes place our Monad will not admit of other units or numbers, because it is self-sufficient, and exactly so, within itself; absolute in all numbers in the amplitude of which it is diffused, not only magically but also by a somewhat vulgar process employed by the artist, which produces great results in dignity and power within this selfsame Monad, which is resolved into its own first matter; whilst that which is foreign to its nature and to its natural hereditary proportions is segregated with the greatest care and diligence and rejected for ever amongst the imputities.

THEOREM XXI

If that which is hidden within the profundities of our Monad be brought to light, or, on the contrary, if those primary parts which are exterior in our Monad are enclosed in the centre, you will see the extent to which the philosophical transformation can be produced. We will now expound to you another local commutation of our mystical Monad, using those parts from the hieroglyphic characters of the superior planets which are immediately offered to us. Each one of the other planets for this purpose is in turn elevated to a position which was frequently assigned to them by Plato, therefore, if they are conveniently taken in this position and at this point in Aries, Saturn and Jupiter are in conjunction. By descending, the Cross represents Venus and Mercury, followed by the Sun himself with the Moon at the bottom. This will be refuted in other circles; meantime, as we have no wish to hide the philosophical treasure of our Monad, we have taken a resolution to give a reason by which the position of the Monad is by this manner displaced. Yet see! listen to these other great secrets which I know and will disclose to assist you as touching this position, which I can explain in few words. We distribute our Monad, now looked at from a different aspect, and analysed in a different manner, as is seen at B, D, C. In this new Ternary the figures C and D are known to all men, but the figure designated B is not easy of comprehension.

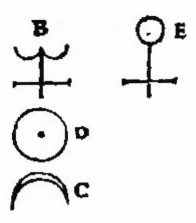

It is necessary to give careful consideration to the known forms D and C, which show that the essences are separated and distinct from the figure B: also we see that the Horns of the figure C are turned downwards towards the Earth. That part of D which illumines C is also towards the Earth, that is to say, downwards, in the centre of which the solitary visible point alone is truly the Earth: finally these two figures D and C turned towards the lower end give a hieroglyphic indication of the Earth. Therefore, the Earth is made to represent, hieroglyphically, stability and fixation. I leave you to judge from this what is meant by C and D: from which you may take notice of a great secret. All the qualities which we have in the first place ascribed to the Sun and the Moon can here be given a perfect and very necessary interpretation, these two stars up to now having been placed in the superior position with the horns of the Moon raised on high; but we have already spoken of this.

We will now examine, according to the fundamentals of our hieroglyphic Art, the nature of this third figure B. First, we carry to the Crown the double crescent of the Moon which is our Aries, turned round in a mystical manner. Then follows the hieroglyphic sign of the Elements, which is attached to it. As to why we use the double Moon, it may be explained that it is according to the matter, which requires a double quantity of the Moon. We speak of those grades of which in their experiments the Philosophers could find no more than four, amongst all created substances, that is to say, to be, to live, to feel and to comprehend (*esse, vivere, sentire et entelligere*). In saying that the first two of these Elements are found here, we say that they are called *argent vive (luna existens, viva)*, all life being subject to movement, there being six principles of movement. The Cross which is attached implies that in this artifice the Elements are requisite. We have told you many times that in our theory the hieroglyph of the Moon is like a semicircle, and on the contrary the complete circle signifies the Sun, whereas here we have two semicircles separated, but touching at a common point; if these are combined, as they can be by a certain art, the product can represent the circular plenitude of the Sun. From all those things which we have considered, the result is that we can summarise, and in hieroglyphic form, offer the following:

Argent vive, which must be developed by the magistery of the Elements, possesses the power of the solar force through the unification of its two semicircles combined by a secret art.

The circle, of which we have spoken and which we designate in the figure by the letter E, is thus accomplished and formed. You will recollect, we have said that the solar degree is not delivered to us ready to our hand by Nature, but that it is artificial and not produced by Nature, it being available to us in its first aspect in accordance with its proper nature (as in B) in two parts separated and dissolved, and not solidly united in the solar body. In fact, the semi-diameter of these half-circles is not equal to the semi-diameter of D and C, but much smaller. Everyone can see this from the manner in which we have drawn them in the diagram, from which it is clear that this same B has not as great an amplitude as D and C. The proportions in the figure confirm this, being by this means transformed into a circle from B into E. Therefore, there appears before our eyes the sign of Venus alone. We have already demonstrated by these hieroglyphical syllogisms that from B we cannot obtain the true D, and that the true C is not and cannot be completely within the nature of B; therefore, this of itself is not able to become the true "Argent Vive." You may already doubt the subject of this life and of this movement, whether it is possible, in fact, to possess it naturally or not. However, as we have already explained to the wise, all those things which are said about B, in a similar manner will be at least analogical, and all that which we have briefly taught concerning C and D can be very well applied, by analogy, to this same B accompanied by its Elements. Indeed, that which we have attached to the nature of Aries, should exactly fit the case, because it carries this figure B, although reversed, at its summit, and that which is attached to the figure B, is the mystical figure of the Elements. Therefore, we see by this anatomy that from the body of our Monad alone, separated in this manner by our Art, this new Ternary is formed.

This we cannot doubt, for the reason that the members which composed it reassemble and form amongst themselves of their own free will a monadic union and sympathy which is absolute. By this means we discover amongst these members a force which is both magnetic and active.

Finally I think it well to note here, by way of recreation, that this same B shows very clearly the same proportions in the malformed and rustic letter in that it carries visible points towards the top and at the front and that these letters are three in number, otherwise they number six, summarising three times three: they are crude and malformed, unstable and inconstant, made in such a manner as to appear formed of a series of half-circles.

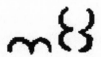

But the method of making these letters more stable and firm is in the hands of the literary experts. I have here placed before your eyes an infinitude of mysteries: I introduce a game but to interrupt a theory. Meanwhile I do not understand the efforts of certain people who rise up against me. Our Monad being reconstituted in its first mystical position and each one of its parts being ordered by Art, I advise and exhort them to search with zeal for that fire of Aries in the first triplicity, which is our equinoctial fire and which is the cause whereby our Sun may be elevated above his vulgar quality. Many other excellent things should also be studied in happy and wise meditations.

We now pass on to another subject; we wish to point the way, not only in a friendly but also in a faithful manner, to those other secrets upon which we must insist, before we lapse into silence and which, as we have said, comprise a most remarkable infinitude of other mysteries.

THEOREM XXII

It will be readily understood that the mysteries of our Monad cannot be extracted unless one is drawn towards the pharmacy of this same Monad, and that these mysteries must not be revealed to any but the Initiates. I offer here for the contemplation of your Serene Highness, the vessels of the Sacred Art which are truly and completely kabbalistic. All those lines which unite the diverse parts of our Monad are most wisely separated; we give to each one of them a special letter, in order to distinguish them one from another as you will see in the diagram.

We inform you that in "oc" [the mark in the upper right hand corner resembling the symbol for Taurus lying on it's side] is found a certain artificial vessel, formed of A and B with the line M. The exterior diameter is common to both A and B, and this is not different, as we see, from this the first letter of the Greek alphabet, except by a single transposition of the parts.

We teach the true mystical sympathy first by the line, the circle, and the semicircle, and, as we have formerly said, this symmetry can only be formed of the circle and the semicircle, which are always joined for the same mystical purpose.

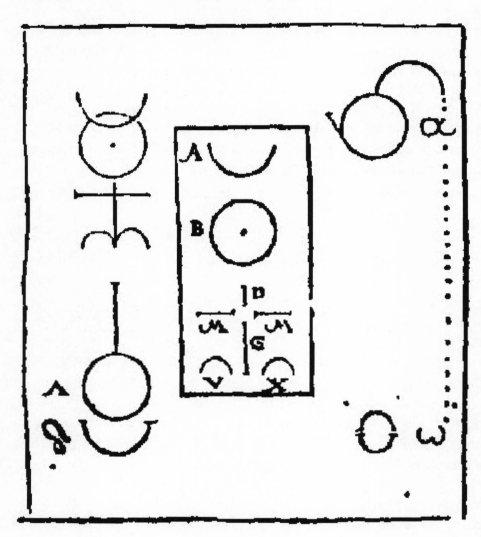

It follows that λ and δ are in themselves the shapes of other vessels. That is to say, λ is made of glass and δ of earth (earthenware or clay). In the second place, λ and δ may remind us of the Pestle and Mortar, which must be made of suitable substance, in which artificial unperforated pearls, lamels of crystal and beryl, chrysolite, precious rubies, carbuncles and other rare artificial stones may be ground to powder.

Lastly, that which is indicated by the letter ω is a small vessel containing the mysteries, which is never far from this last letter of the Greek alphabet now restored to its primitive mystagogy, and which is made by a single transposition of its component parts, consisting of two half-circles of equal size. Concerning the vulgar objects and necessities which are required in addition to the vessels, and the materials out of which they should be fashioned, it would be useless that we should treat of it here.

Meanwhile α must be considered as if searching for the occasion to perform its function by a very secret and rapid spiral circulation and an incorruptible salt by which the first principle of all things is preserved, or better, that the substance which floats within the vitriol after its dissolution, shows the apprentice a primordial but very transitory specimen of our work, and if he is attentive, a very subtle and most effective way to prepare the work will be revealed to him.

Within λ, the glass vessel, during the exercise of its particular function, all air must be excluded or it will be extremely prejudicial. The corollary of ω is the agreeable man, ready, active, and well disposed at all times.

Corollary.

Who, then, is not now able to procure the sweet and salutary fruits of this Science, which, I say, spring from the mystery of these two letters?

Some of those who would draw us away from our Garden of the Hesperides, and would make us view this a little closer as in a mirror, say that it is established that it is not formed from anything but out Monad.

But the straight line which appears in Alpha is homologous with that which, in the separation of the final analysis of our Cross, is already designated by the letter M. One may discover by these means from where the others are produced. See the scheme outlined in the table:

	Exiftens ante Elementa.	Adam Mortalis Mafculus & Fœmina.	Morifi-cans	Adumbra-tus.	Natus in Stabolo.
	Elemetaris œconomia.	Elemétalis Genealogic Confum-matio.	Crux.	Crux.	Holocau-ftum in Cruce
	Exiftens poft Elementa.	ADAM IMMOR-TALIS.	Vivificans.	Manifeftif-fimus.	Rex Regum Vbique.
Conceptus Singularida-fluentis.	Potentiæ Semen.	Creatio Hylæ.	Matrimo-nium Ter-reftre.	Principium	
Paffus & Se-pultus.	יהוה Virtus Denaria.	Depuratio Elementalis.	Crucis Martyrii.	Medium.	
Refurgens, propria vir-tute.	Gloriæ Triüphus.	Transfor-matio.	Matrimo-nium Divinum.	Finis.	

In these few words, I know that I give not only the principles but the demonstration to those who can see in them how to fortify the igneous vigour and the celestial origin, so that they may lend a willing ear to the great Democritus, certain that it is not mythical dogma but mystic and secret, according to which it is the medicine of the soul, the liberator from all suffering, and is prepared for those who wish for it and as he has taught; it is to be sought for in the Voice of the Creator of the Universe, so that men, inspired by God, and engendered anew, learn through the perfect disquisition of the mystical languages.

THEOREM XXIII

We now present in diagrammatic form the proportions already observed by us in the hieroglyphic construction of our Monad, which must be observed by those who wish to engrave them upon their seals or their rings, or to utilise them in some other manner. In the name of Jesus Christ crucified upon the Cross, I say the Spirit writes these things rapidly through me; I hope, and I believe, I am merely the quill which traces these characters. The Spirit draws us now towards our Cross of the Elements, with all the following measures which are also to be obtained by a reasoning process according to the subject-matter which it is proposed to discuss. Everything which exists under the heaven of the Moon contains the principle of its own generation within itself and is formed from the coagulation of the four Elements, unless it be the primary substance itself, and this in several ways not known to the vulgar, there being nothing in the created world in which the Elements are in equal proportion

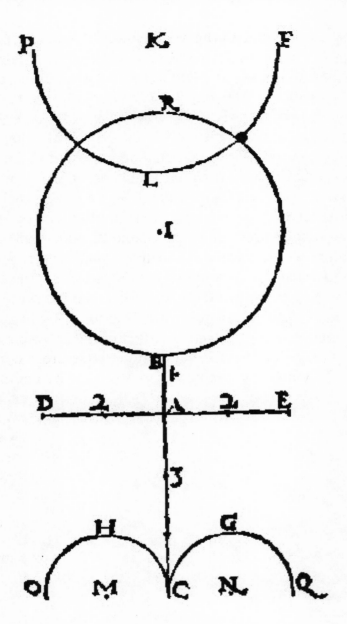

or in equal force. But by means of our Art, they can be restored to equality in certain respects, as the wise well know; therefore, in our Cross, we make the parts equal and unequal.

Another reason is that we can proclaim either similitude, or diversity, or unity, or plurality in affirming the secret properties of the equilateral Cross, as we have said before.

If we were to expound all the reasons which we know, for the proportions established in this way, or if we were to demonstrate the causes by another method which we have not done, although we have done so sufficiently for the Sages, we should transcend the limits of obscurity which we have prescribed, not without reason, for our discourse.

Take any point, as A for example, draw a straight line through it in both directions, as CAK. Divide the line CK at A by a line at right angles, which we will call DAE. Now select a point anywhere on the line AK, let it be B, and one obtains the primary measurement of AB, which will be the common measure of our work. Take three times the length of AB and mark off the central line from A to C, which will be AC. Now take twice the distance between AB and mark it off on the line DAE at E and again at D, in such a way that the distance between D and E is four times the distance between A and B. Thus is formed our Cross of four Elements, that is to say, the Quaternary formed by the lines AB, AC, AD, AE. Now on the line BK take a distance equal to AD up the central line to I. With this point I as a centre, and IB as the radius, describe a circle which cuts the line AK at R: from the point R towards K mark a distance equal to AB, let it be RK. From the point K draw a line at right angles to the central line on both sides, forming an angle on either side of AK, which will be PFK. From the point K measure in the direction of F a distance equal to AD, which will be KF: now with K as centre and KF as radius describe a half-circle FLP, so that FKP is the diameter. Finally, at point C draw a line at right angles to AC sufficiently long in both directions to form OCQ. Now on the line CO we measure from C a distance equal to AB, which is CM, and with M as a centre and MC as a radius we describe a semicircle CHO. And in the same manner on CQ, from the point C we measure a distance equal to AB which is CN, and from the centre N, with CN as radius, we trace a semicircle CGQ, of which CNQ is the diameter. We now affirm, from this, that all the requisite measurements are found explained and described in our Monad.

It would be well to notice, you who know the distances of our mechanism, that the whole of the line CK is composed of nine parts, of which one is our fundamental, and which in another fashion is able to contribute towards the perfection of our work: then, again, all the diameters and semi-diameters must be designated here by suppositional lines hidden or obscured, as the geometricians say. It is not necessary to leave any centre visible, the exception being the solar centre, which is here marked by the letter I, to which it is unnecessary to add any letter. Meanwhile those who are adept at our mechanism can add something to the solar periphery, by way of ornament and not by virtue of any mystical necessity: for this reason it has not been formerly considered by us. This something is a boundary ring, necessarily a line parallel to the original periphery. The distance between these parallels may be fixed at a quarter or a fifth part of the distance AB. One may also give to the crescent of the Moon a form which this planet frequently assumes in the sky, after her conjunction with the Sun -- that is to say, in the form of the Horns, which you will obtain if from the point K in the direction of R you measure the distance just mentioned, *i.e.* the fourth or fifth part of the line AB, and if from the point thereby obtained, as a centre, you trace with the original lunar radius the second part of the lunar crescent, which joins the extremities at both ends of the first semicircle. You may perform a similar operation in respect of the positions M and N when erecting the perpendicular at each one of these centre points; we can use the sixth part of AB or a little less, from which point, as the centre, we describe two other semicircles, using the radius of the two first, MC and NC.

Lastly, the parallels may be traced at each side of the two lines of our Cross, each side at a distance from the centre line of one-eighth to one-tenth part of the distance AB, in such a way that our Cross be in this manner formed into four superficial lines where the width is the fourth or the fifth part of this same line AB.

I have wished in some way to sketch these ornaments in the figure which each one may reproduce according to his own fancy. It is a condition, however, that you do not commit any fault, however small, against the mystical symmetry for fear of introducing by your negligence a new discipline into these hieroglyphic measurements; for it is very necessary that during the succeeding progression in time they must be neither disturbed nor destroyed. This is much more profound than we are able to indicate, even if we wished to do so, in this small book, for we teach Truth, the daughter of Time, God willing.

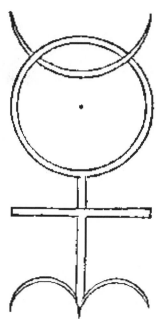

We will now expound methodically certain things which you may find on your way by practising the proportions of our Monad. Then we will show by many examples the existence of four lines corresponding to the four lines of our Cross, and which in this consideration we are not able simply to announce, because of the proportions and the particular and mystical results which are produced in another fashion, from the Quaternary of these same lines. And thirdly, we will show that there exist within Nature certain useful functions determined by God by means of numbers, which we have happily obtained and which are explained either in this theorem, or in others, contained in this little book.

Finally, we will insert other things in an opportune place which, if they are conveniently understood, will produce fruits most abundantly.

We now abruptly conclude.

	24 possible permutations.
Of the Pythagorean quaternary	The Pythagorean sum is 10.

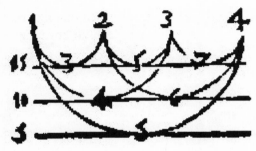

A complete addition of the parts yields 30.

Take the same proportion which is shown in numbers when written in the natural order, after the first Monad, then from the first to the last make a continuous multiplication -- that is to say, the first by the second, the product of these two by the third, and this product by the fourth, and so on until the last; the final product determines all the Metatheses possible, in respect of the proportion in space, and for the same reason in proportion to diverse objects as you wish.

I tell thee, O King, this operation will be useful unto thee in many circumstances, whether in the study of Nature or in the affairs of the government of men; for it is that which I am accustomed to use with the greatest of pleasure in the Tziruph or Themura of the Hebrews.

Of the artificial quaternary

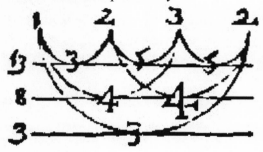

- a continuous multiplication yields 12.
- a simple addition yields 8. (1, 7; 4, 3)
- the sum of a complete addition of the parts is -- 24, a number which is the same in any possible transposition of the quaternary, and which designates the physical purity and highest quality of gold, (namely that) of

24 carat when one has it,
by itself, above ground.

I know that many other powerful numbers may be produced out of
our Quaternary, by virtue of arithmetic and the power of numbers.
Yet he who does not understand that a very great obscurity has by
this method been illuminated by those numbers which I have
drawn out which have nature and distinction amongst such a
multitude, will not be able to estimate their meaning, which is
obscure and not to the point. How many will find in our numbers
the authority which we have promised for the weight of the
Elements; for the statements regarding measurements of time; and
for the certainty of proportions which may be assigned to the
powers and forces of things? All this you should study in the two
preceding diagrams.

Many things may be deduced from the diagrams which, it is
preferable, should be studied silently rather than divulged openly
in words. Meantime, let us inform you of one thing, amongst
many others, disclosed now for the first time by us, in respect of

this new Art; to wit, we have here established a rational cause by virtue of which the Quaternary with the Decad, in a certain manner, terminate the numerical series. We affirm that this cause is not exactly that which was described by the Masters who have preceded us, but just as we have stated it here. This Monad has been integrally and physically restored to itself -- that is to say, it is truly the Monad Unitissima, the proved unity of the images; and it is not within the power of Nature, neither can we by any art promote in it any movement or any progression whatsoever, unless it be by four super-celestial cycles or revolutions, and from this Monad is engendered that which we wish to note as the manner and course of its eminence; and for this reason, that there is not in the elemental world, nor in the celestial or super-celestial worlds, any created power or influence which cannot be absolutely favoured and enriched by it.

It was because of the true effect of this that four illustrious men, friends of Philosophy, were upon an occasion together in the great work. One day they were astonished by a great miracle in this thing, and forthwith dedicated themselves from that day forward to sing praises to God and to preach the thrice Mighty because He had given them so much wisdom and power and so great an Empire over all other creatures.

THEOREM XXIV

Just as we commenced the first theorem of this little book with the point, the straight line, and the circle, and have extended it from the Monadic point to the extreme linear efflux of the Elements in a circle, almost analogous to the equinoctial which makes one revolution in 24 hours, so now at last we consummate and terminate the metamorphosis and the metathesis of all possible contents of the Quaternary defined by the number 24 by our present twenty-fourth theorem, to the honour and Glory of Him, as witnesseth John the Archpraesul of the Divine Mysteries, in the fourth and last part of the fourth chapter of the Apocalypse, who is seated on His Throne, around and in front of which the four animals, each with six wings, chant night and day without repose: "Holy, Holy, Holy is the Lord God Omnipotent, who was, is and is to come," the same as the 24 ancient ones in the 24 seats placed in the circle, adore Him and prostrate themselves, having cast their Crowns of gold to earth, saying: "Worthy art Thou, O God, to receive Glory, Honour, and Virtue, because Thou hast created all things, and out of Thy Will they have been created."

Amen, says the fourth letter.

Δ :

He to whom God has given the will and the ability to know in this way the Divine mystery through the eternal monuments of literature and to finish with great tranquillity this work on the 25th January, having commenced it on the 13th of the same month.

In the year 1564 at Antwerp.

Here the vulgar eye will see nothing but Obscurity and will despair considerably.

Manufactured by Amazon.ca
Bolton, ON